W9-CHI-116

STEP-BY-STEP

Chinese Cantonese Cooking

STEP-BY-STEP

Chinese Cantonese Cooking

DEH–TA HSIUNG

SHOOTING STAR PRESS

This edition printed in 1995 for:
Shooting Star Press Inc
230 Fifth Avenue – Suite 1212
New York, NY 10001

Shooting Star Press books are available at special discounts for bulk purchases for sales promotions, premiums, fund-raising, or educational use. Special edition or book excerpts can also be created to specification. For details contact: Special Sales Director, Shooting Star Press Inc., 230 Fifth Avenue, Suite 1212, New York, NY 10001

© Parragon Book Service Ltd 1994

ISBN 1 56924 192 9

All rights reserved. No part of the publication may be reproduced, stored in a retrieval system, or transmitted in any way or by any means, electronic, mechanical, photocopy, recording or otherwise, without the prior permission of the copyright holder.

Printed in Italy

Acknowledgements:

Design & DTP: Pedro & Frances Prá-Lopez / Kingfisher Design
Art Direction: Pedro Prá-Lopez
Managing Editor: Alexa Stace
Photography: Amanda Heywood
Cover Photography: Clive Streeter
Cover Step-by-Step Photography: Karl Adamson
Home Economist: Deh-Ta Hsiung
Stylist: Marian Price

Gas Hob supplied by New World Domestic Appliances Ltd
Photographs on pages 6, 18, 26, 56 & 66: Tony Stone Images

Contents

❧

CHAPTER ONE

Appetizers

A number of dishes in Cantonese cooking are served as an appetizer – just like hors d'oeuvres in the West. One of the advantages of these dishes is that they are generally prepared and cooked well in advance – hours or even days before serving. Also, almost all the dishes selected here are ideal for a buffet-style meal or as party food. Instead of serving different appetizers individually, try serving a small portion of each together as an assorted hors d'oeuvres. Select a minimum of three or four different items: Crispy Egg Rolls, Butterfly Shrimp, Barbecue Spare Ribs, Barbecue Pork (Char Siu), and so on.

Other dishes from the Main Course section that can be served as a part of the appetizer are Sweet and Sour Shrimp, Lemon Chicken, and Baked Crab with Ginger, and Scallions. Remember not to have more than one of the same type of food – the ingredients should be chosen for their harmony and balance in color, aroma, flavor and texture.

Opposite: *A Chinese cook at an open-air stall in Xinjiang province. Wayside stalls selling takeout food are a common sight all over China, offering wontons, spare ribs, shrimp, egg rolls, and other tasty snacks for hungry workers.*

STEP 3

STEP 4

STEP 5

STEP 6

CRISPY VEGETARIAN EGG ROLLS

For a non-vegetarian version, just replace mushrooms with chicken or pork, and the carrots with shrimp.

MAKES 12 ROLLS

1⅓ *cups fresh bean sprouts, washed and drained*
1-2 scallions
1 medium carrot
⅓ *cup canned sliced bamboo shoots, rinsed and drained*
1 cup mushrooms
2-3 tbsp vegetable oil, plus oil for deep-frying
½ *tsp salt*
½ *tsp sugar*
1 tbsp light soy sauce
1 tsp Chinese rice wine or dry sherry
12 egg roll skins, defrosted if frozen
1 tbsp cornstarch paste (see page 77)
flour, for dusting
vegetable oil, for deep-frying

1 Cut all the vegetables into thin shreds roughly the same size and shape as the bean sprouts.

2 Heat the oil in a hot wok and stir-fry the vegetables for about 1 minute. Add the salt, sugar, soy sauce, and wine and continue stirring for 1½-2 minutes. Remove the vegetables from the wok with a slotted spoon and place in a bowl. Drain off the excess liquid, then leave to cool.

3 To make the egg rolls, place about 2 tablespoons of the vegetables one-third of the way down on a skin, with the triangle pointing away from you.

4 Lift the lower flap over the filling and fold in one end.

5 Roll once and fold in the other end.

6 Roll once more, brush the upper edge with a little flour paste, and roll into a neat package. Lightly dust a tray with flour and place the egg roll with the flap-side down. Make the rest of the egg rolls in the same way.

7 Heat the oil in a wok or deep-fryer until smoking, then reduce the heat to low and deep-fry the egg rolls in batches for 2-3 minutes or until golden and crispy. Remove with a slotted spoon and drain on paper towels. Serve hot with a dip sauce such as soy sauce, sweet-and-sour sauce or chili sauce.

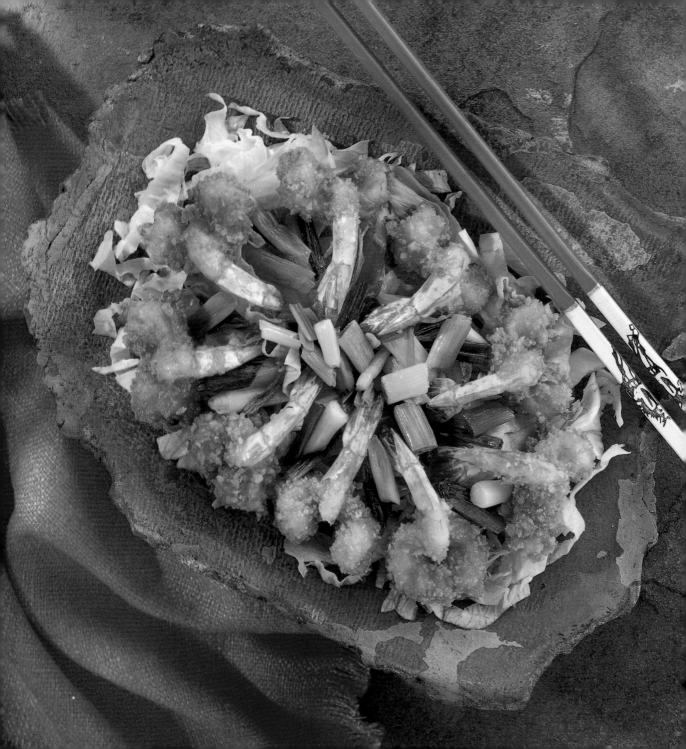

BUTTERFLY SHRIMP

Use unpeeled, raw king or tiger shrimp, which are about 3-4in long.

STEP 1a

STEP 1b

SERVES 4

12 raw tiger shrimp in their shells
2 tbsp light soy sauce
1 tbsp Chinese rice wine or dry sherry
1 tbsp cornstarch
2 eggs, lightly beaten
8-10 tbsp breadcrumbs
vegetable oil, for deep-frying
salt and pepper
shredded lettuce leaves, to serve
chopped scallions, to garnish

1 Shell and devein the shrimp but leave the tails on. Split them in half from the underbelly about halfway along, leaving the tails still firmly attached.

2 Mix together the salt, pepper, soy sauce, wine and cornstarch in a bowl, add the shrimp and turn to coat. Leave to marinate for about 10-15 minutes.

3 Heat the oil in a preheated wok. Pick up each shrimp by the tail, dip it in the beaten egg, then roll it in the breadcrumbs to coat well.

4 Deep-fry the shrimp in batches until golden brown. Remove them with a slotted spoon and drain on paper towels.

5 To serve, arrange the shrimp neatly on a bed of lettuce leaves and garnish with scallions, either raw or soaked for about 30 seconds in hot oil.

VARIATIONS

Butterfly shrimp may also be served on a bed of crispy seaweed. This classic Chinese accompaniment provides the perfect foil for the luscious shrimp. Dried seaweed can be bought in packets from Oriental stores and supermarkets. Follow the instructions on the packet to prepare the seaweed.

TO DEVEIN LARGE SHRIMP

First remove the shell. Make a shallow cut about three-quarters of the way along the back of each shrimp, then pull out and discard the black intestinal vein.

STEP 3a

STEP 3b

STEP 1

STEP 2

STEP 3

STEP 4

LETTUCE-WRAPPED CHOPPED MEAT

The original version of this recipe uses quail or pigeon meat.
Serve the chopped meat and lettuce leaves on separate dishes:
each guest then wraps his or her own parcel.

SERVES 4

1¹/₂ cups chopped or shredded pork or
chicken
1 tbsp finely chopped Chinese mushrooms
1 tbsp finely chopped water chestnuts
salt and pepper
pinch of sugar
1 tsp light soy sauce
1 tsp Chinese rice wine or dry sherry
1 tsp cornstarch
2-3 tbsp vegetable oil
¹/₂ tsp finely chopped ginger root
1 tsp finely chopped scallions
1 tbsp finely chopped Szechuan preserved
vegetables (optional)
1 tbsp oyster sauce
a few drops of sesame oil
8 crisp lettuce leaves, to serve

1 Mix the meat with the mushrooms, water chestnuts, salt, pepper, sugar, soy sauce, wine, and cornstarch.

2 Heat the oil in a preheated wok or skillet and add the ginger and scallions followed by the meat. Stir-fry for 1 minute.

3 Add the Szechuan preserved vegetables and continue stirring for 1 more minute. Add the oyster sauce and sesame oil, blend well and cook for 1 more minute. Remove to a warmed serving dish.

4 To serve: place about 2-3 tablespoons of the mixture on a lettuce leaf and roll it up tightly to form a small parcel. Eat with your fingers.

SZECHUAN PRESERVED VEGETABLES

These pickled mustard roots are hot and salty, with a peppery flavor, and are often used to intensify the spiciness of a dish. Once opened, store in the refrigerator in a tightly sealed jar.

STEP 1

STEP 2

STEP 3

STEP 4

BARBECUE SPARE RIBS

This is a simplified version of the half saddle of pork ribs seen hanging in the windows of Cantonese restaurants. Use the specially small, thin ribs known as finger ribs.

SERVES 4
OVEN: 450°F
THEN 400°F

1 lb pork finger spare ribs
1 tbsp sugar
1 tbsp light soy sauce
1 tbsp dark soy sauce
3 tbsp hoi-sin sauce
1 tbsp rice wine or dry sherry
4-5 tbsp water or Chinese Stock (see page 76)
mild chili sauce, to dip
cilantro leaves, to garnish

1 Trim off any excess fat from the ribs and cut into pieces. Mix the ribs with the sugar, light and dark soy sauce, hoi-sin sauce, and wine in a baking dish, and marinate for about 2-3 hours.

2 Add the water or stock to the ribs and spread them out in the dish. Roast in a preheated hot oven for 15 minutes.

3 Turn the ribs over, lower the heat and cook for 30-35 minutes longer.

4 To serve, chop each rib into 3-4 small, bite-sized pieces with a large knife or Chinese cleaver and arrange on a serving dish. Pour the sauce from the baking dish over them, garnish with cilantro leaves, and serve with chili sauce as a dip.

HOI-SIN SAUCE

This sweet, thick sauce is made from soybean flour, soy beans, vinegar, sesame seed oil, chili, sugar, salt, garlic, and spices. It is sold in cans and jars; if you buy it in a can, store it in a glass bottle in the refrigerator once opened, where it will keep for several months. It is ideal for use in marinades and as a dip or condiment for many Chinese dishes.

SPARE RIBS

Ask the butcher to cut some if you can't find the right size of ribs on the shelf. Don't throw away any trimmings from the ribs – they can be used for soup or stock.

14

STEP 1

STEP 2

STEP 4

STEP 5

BARBECUE PORK (CHAR SIU)

Also called honey-roasted pork, these are the strips of reddish meat sometimes seen hanging in the windows of Cantonese restaurants.

SERVES 4
OVEN: 425°F
THEN 350°F

1 lb pork tenderloin
²/₃ cup boiling water
1 tbsp honey, dissolved with a little hot
   water

MARINADE:
1 tbsp sugar
1 tbsp crushed yellow bean sauce
1 tbsp light soy sauce
1 tbsp hoi-sin sauce
1 tbsp oyster sauce
¹/₂ tsp chili sauce
1 tbsp brandy or rum
1 tsp sesame oil
shredded lettuce, to serve

1 Cut the pork into strips about 1 in thick and 7-8 in long and place in a large shallow dish. Add the marinade ingredients and turn the pork until well coated. Cover, and leave to marinate for at least 3-4 hours, turning occasionally.

2 Remove the pork strips from the dish with a slotted spoon, reserving the marinade. Arrange the pork strips on a rack over a baking pan. Place the pan in the preheated oven and pour in the boiling water. Roast for about 10-15 minutes.

3 Lower the oven temperature. Baste the pork strips with the reserved marinade and turn. Roast for a further 10 minutes.

4 Remove the pork from the oven, brush with the honey syrup, and lightly brown under a medium hot broiler for 3-4 minutes, turning once or twice.

5 To serve, allow the pork to cool slightly before cutting it. Cut across the grain into thin slices and arrange on a bed of shredded lettuce. Make a sauce by boiling the marinade and the drippings in the baking pan for a few minutes, strain and pour over the pork.

CHAPTER TWO

Soups

Soup is not normally served as a separate course in China, except at formal occasions and banquets – and then it usually appears towards the end of the meal.

At an everyday meal in Chinese homes, a simply made soup, almost always a clear broth in which a small amount of thinly sliced or shredded vegetables and/or meat have been poached quickly, is served with the other dishes in the meal.

If a good stock is not available, as is often the case in Chinese homes, a Chinese housewife would just stir-fry the ingredients first in a little oil, then add water and seasonings (salt, soy sauce or monosodium glutamate) to make an instant soup fit for the gods!

If you use a chicken bouillon cube, remember to reduce the amount of seasonings in the recipes, since most commercially made bouillon cubes are fairly salty and spicy. It is always worth making your own Chinese Stock (see page 76) if you have the time.

Opposite: *Father and son enjoy a bowl of soup with wontons in a Shanghai restaurant. In China soup is usually served with other dishes as part of a meal, not a separate course as in the West.*

SWEETCORN & CRAB MEAT SOUP

*You must use creamed corn for this soup, which originated in America.
Chicken can be used instead of the crab meat, if preferred.*

STEP 1

SERVES 4

¹/₂ cup crab meat
¹/₄ tsp finely chopped ginger root
2 egg whites
2 tbsp milk
1 tbsp cornstarch paste (see page 77)
2 ¹/₂ cups Chinese Stock (see page 76)
1 x 8-oz can creamed corn
salt and pepper
finely chopped scallions, to garnish

adjust the seasoning and stir gently until
the mixture is well blended. Serve hot,
garnished with chopped scallions.

STEP 2

1 Flake the crab meat (or coarsely
chop the chicken breast) and mix
with the ginger.

2 Beat the egg whites until frothy,
add the milk and cornstarch paste
and beat again until smooth. Blend in the
crab or chicken.

3 In a wok or large skillet, bring the
stock to the boil, add the creamed
corn and bring back to the boil once
more.

4 Stir in the crab meat or chicken
pieces and egg-white mixture,

CHOOSING CRAB

Always obtain the freshest possible crab;
fresh is best, though frozen or canned will
work for this recipe. The delicate, sweet
flavor of crab diminishes quickly: this is
why many Chinese cooks make a point of
buying live crab.

CREAMED CORN

Although sweetcorn is not unknown in
Asia today, it really is a Western food by
tradition. Be sure to use proper creamed
corn for this soup, as it has quite a
different texture from the more usual corn
kernels. Creamed corn has a thick, slightly
mushy consistency, making a thick,
creamy soup.

STEP 3

STEP 4

STEP 1

STEP 2

STEP 3

STEP 5

SEAFOOD & TOFU SOUP

Use shrimp, squid or scallops, or a combination of all three.

SERVES 4

*1¹/₂ cups seafood: peeled shrimp, squid,
   scallops, etc., defrosted if frozen
¹/₂ egg white, lightly beaten
1 tbsp cornstarch paste (see page 77)
1 cake tofu (bean curd), about 3 in square
3 cups Chinese Stock (see page 76)
1 tbsp light soy sauce
salt and pepper
fresh cilantro leaves, to garnish (optional)*

1 Small shrimp can be left whole;
larger ones should be cut into
smaller pieces; cut the squid and scallops
into small pieces.

2 If raw, mix the shrimp and
scallops with the egg white and
cornstarch paste to prevent them from
becoming tough when they are cooked.

3 Cut the cake of tofu into about 24
small cubes.

4 Bring the stock to a rolling boil.
Add the tofu and soy sauce, bring
back to the boil and simmer for 1
minute.

5 Stir in the seafood, raw pieces first,
precooked ones last. Bring back to
boil and simmer for just 1 minute. Adjust
the seasoning and serve garnished with
cilantro leaves, if liked.

FRESH CILANTRO

The musky, sharp scent and flavor of fresh
cilantro is truly distinctive. When buying it
fresh, look for bright green, unwilted
leaves. To store it, wash and dry the
leaves and leave them on the stem. Wrap
the leaves in damp paper towels and keep
them in a plastic bag in the refrigerator.

TOFU

Tofu, also known as bean curd, is an
almost tasteless substance made from
puréed yellow soy beans, which are
very high in protein. It is widely available
in supermarkets, and Oriental and health-
food stores. It is sold in cakes about
3 in square.

STEP 1

STEP 2

STEP 3

STEP 4

MIXED VEGETABLE SOUP

Select 3 or 4 of the suggested vegetables for this soup: the Chinese like to blend different colors, flavors and textures in order to create harmony as well as contrast.

SERVES 4

equal amounts, about ¹/₂- 1 cup each, of mushrooms, carrots, asparagus, snow peas, bamboo shoots, baby sweetcorn, cucumber, tomatoes, spinach, lettuce, Chinese cabbage, bean curd
2¹/₂ cups Chinese Stock (see page 76)
1 tbsp light soy sauce
a few drops of sesame oil (optional)
salt and pepper
finely chopped scallions, to garnish

1 Cut your selection of vegetables into roughly uniform shapes and sizes (slices, shreds or cubes, as you prefer).

2 Bring the stock to a rolling boil in a wok and add the vegetables, bearing in mind that some vegetables require a longer cooking time than others: add carrots and baby sweetcorn first, cook for 2 minutes, then add asparagus, mushrooms, Chinese cabbage, bean curd, and cook for another minute.

3 Spinach, lettuce, watercress, cucumber, and tomato are added last. Stir, and bring the soup back to the boil.

4 Add soy sauce and sesame oil, and adjust the seasoning. Serve hot, garnished with scallions.

SESAME OIL

Sesame oil is a low-saturate oil widely used for its nutty, aromatic flavor. This rich-flavored oil is made from the toasted sesame seeds and used as a seasoning, not as a cooking oil. Thick and dark, it burns easily, so it should be added at the last moment, just before serving. It makes a wonderful dressing for salads when diluted with other vegetable oils. A few drops are often added to soups and other dishes just before serving – it can often be seen on the surface, as in the photograph opposite.

CHAPTER THREE

Main Course Dishes

The main course dishes in a conventional Chinese meal are usually stir-fried or braised. Certain dishes may require a longer cooking time and, strictly speaking, belong to a separate course – known as the principal dish – and should be served independently.

Stir-frying meat and fish dishes have become very popular in Western kitchens in recent years. This is because these dishes are comparatively simple and easy to prepare and cook, as well as being economical, delicious and healthy. Basically, the ingredients are cut into small, thin slices or shreds, then tossed and stirred in hot oil over high heat for a very short time. Thus the natural flavors, as well as the subtle textures, of the food are preserved. When correctly done, the meats (which include fish and poultry) should be tender and juicy, and the vegetables crisp and bright – over-cooking will render the food into a tasteless soggy mess.

Opposite: *Work is finished for the day, and a cook in XinJiang sells noodles for the evening meal. It takes years to learn the art of making noodles and the products of specialist noodle-makers are greatly sought after.*

SWEET-&-SOUR SHRIMP

*Use raw shrimp if possible; ready-cooked ones can be added to the
sauce without the initial deep-frying (step 2).*

STEP 1

STEP 2

STEP 3

STEP 4

SERVES 4

*1²/₃-2 cups raw king or tiger shrimp in their
  shells
vegetable oil, for deep-frying
fresh cilantro leaves, to garnish*

SAUCE:
*1 tbsp vegetable oil
2 tsp finely chopped scallions
1 tsp finely chopped ginger root
1 tbsp light soy sauce
2 tbsp sugar
3 tbsp rice vinegar
1 tsp Chinese rice wine or dry sherry
¹/₂ cup Chinese Stock (see page 76) or water
1 tbsp cornstarch paste (see page 77)
a few drops of sesame oil
cilantro leaves, to garnish*

1 Remove the legs from the shrimp
but leave the body shell.

2 Heat the oil in a preheated wok.
Deep-fry the shrimp in hot oil for
about 45-50 seconds, or until they
become bright orange. Remove
with a slotted spoon and drain on
paper towels.

3 To make the sauce, heat the oil in a
preheated wok and add the
scallions and ginger, followed by the
seasonings, sugar and stock or water.
Bring to the boil.

4 Add the shrimp to the sauce, blend
well, then thicken the sauce with
the cornstarch paste. Stir until smooth
and add the sesame oil.

5 Serve hot, garnished with cilantro
leaves.

SWEET-AND-SOUR
SAUCE

It is now possible to buy ready-made
sweet-and-sour sauce in bottles. They are
really handy if you are short of time, but
they are no match for the homemade
version, which has a much subtler flavor.

STEP 2

STEP 3

STEP 4

STEP 5

FRIED SQUID FLOWERS

The addition of green bell pepper and black bean sauce to the squid makes a colorful and delicious dish from the Cantonese school.

SERVES 4

12-14 oz prepared and cleaned squid (see below)
1 medium green bell pepper, cored and seeded
3-4 tbsp vegetable oil
1 garlic clove, finely chopped
$1/4$ tsp finely chopped ginger root
2 tsp finely chopped scallions
$1/2$ tsp salt
2 tbsp crushed black bean sauce
1 tsp Chinese rice wine or dry sherry
a few drops of sesame oil

1 If ready-prepared squid is not available, prepare as instructed below right.

2 Open up the squid and score the inside of the flesh in a criss-cross pattern.

3 Cut the squid into pieces about the size of an oblong postage stamp. Blanch in a bowl of boiling water for a few seconds. Remove and drain; dry well on paper towels.

4 Cut the bell pepper into small triangular pieces. Heat the oil in a preheated wok and stir-fry the bell pepper for about 1 minute. Add the garlic, ginger, scallions, salt and squid. Continue stirring for another minute.

5 Finally add the black bean sauce and wine, and blend well. Serve hot, sprinkled with sesame oil.

TO CLEAN THE SQUID

Clean the squid by first cutting off the head. Cut off the tentacles and reserve. Remove the small soft bone at the base of the tentacles and the transparant backbone, as well as the ink bag. Peel off the thin skin, then wash and dry well.

STIR-FRIED SHRIMP

*This colorful and delicious dish is cooked with vegetables:
vary them according to seasonal availability.*

STEP 1

SERVES 4

²/₃ cup snow peas
¹/₂ small carrot, thinly sliced
8 baby sweetcorn
1 cup straw mushrooms
1 - 1¹/₃ cups raw tiger shrimp, peeled
1 tsp salt
¹/₂ egg white, lightly beaten
1 tsp cornstarch paste (see page 77)
about 1¹/₄ cups vegetable oil
1 scallion, cut into short sections
4 slices ginger root, peeled and finely
    chopped
¹/₂ tsp sugar
1 tbsp light soy sauce
1 tsp Chinese rice wine or dry sherry
a few drops of sesame oil

3 Heat a wok over high heat for 2-3 minutes, then add the oil and heat to medium hot before adding the shrimp; stir to separate them. Remove with a slotted spoon as soon as the color changes.

4 Pour off the oil, leaving about 1 tablespoon in the wok. Add all the vegetables and stir-fry for about 1 minute. Add the shrimp and the seasonings. Blend well. Sprinkle with the sesame oil and serve hot.

STEP 2

STEP 3

1 Top and tail the snow peas; cut the carrot into the same size as the snow peas; halve the baby sweetcorn and straw mushrooms.

2 Mix the shrimp with a pinch of the salt, the egg white, and cornstarch paste.

VEGETABLE SELECTION

When choosing alternative vegetables, remember to select contrasting colors and textures, as shown here – one green, one orange, one yellow, etc.

STEP 4

STEP 1

STEP 2

STEP 3

STEP 4

BAKED CRAB WITH GINGER

The crab is interchangeable with lobster. In Chinese restaurants, only live crabs and lobsters are used, but ready-cooked ones can be used at home quite successfully.

SERVES 4

1 large or 2 medium crabs, weighing about
    1½ lb in total
2 tbsp Chinese rice wine or dry sherry
1 egg, lightly beaten
1 tbsp cornstarch
3-4 tbsp vegetable oil
1 tbsp finely chopped ginger root
3-4 scallions, cut into short sections
2 tbsp light soy sauce
1 tsp sugar
about ⅓ cup Chinese Stock (see page 76)
    or water
½ tsp sesame oil
cilantro leaves, to garnish

1 Cut the crab in half from the under-belly. Break off the claws and crack them with the back of the cleaver or a large kitchen knife.

2 Discard the legs and crack the shell, breaking it into several pieces. Discard the feathery gills and the stomach sac. Place in a bowl with the wine, egg and cornstarch and leave to marinate for 10-15 minutes.

3 Heat the oil in a preheated wok and stir-fry the crab with ginger and scallions for 2-3 minutes.

4 Add the soy sauce, sugar and stock or water, blend well and bring to the boil. Cover and cook for 3-4 minutes, then remove the cover, sprinkle with sesame oil and serve.

TECHNIQUES

The term "baked" may be used on Chinese restaurant menus to describe dishes such as this one, which are actually cooked in a wok. "Pot-roasted" may be a more accurate way to describe this cooking technique.

BUYING CRABS

Crabs are almost always sold ready-cooked. The crab should feel heavy for its size, and when it is shaken, there should be no sound of water inside. A good medium-sized crab should yield about 1 lb meat, enough for 3-4 people.

FISH WITH BLACK BEAN SAUCE

Any firm and delicate fish steaks such as salmon, and turbot can be cooked by the same method.

SERVES 4-6

1 sea bass, trout or turbot, weighing about
   1¹/₂ lb, cleaned
1 tsp salt
1 tbsp sesame oil
2-3 scallions, cut in half lengthways
1 tbsp light soy sauce
1 tbsp Chinese rice wine or dry sherry
1 tbsp finely shredded ginger root
1 tbsp oil
2 tbsp crushed black bean sauce
2 finely shredded scallions
fresh cilantro leaves, to garnish (optional)
lemon slices, to garnish

1 Score both sides of the fish with diagonal cuts at 1 in intervals. Rub both the inside and outside of the fish with salt and sesame oil.

2 Place the fish on top of the scallions on a heatproof platter. Blend the soy sauce and wine with the ginger shreds and pour evenly all over the fish.

3 Place the fish on the platter in a very hot steamer (or inside a wok on a rack), cover and steam vigorously for 12-15 minutes.

4 Heat the oil until hot, then blend in the black bean sauce. Remove the fish from the steamer and place on a serving dish. Pour the hot black bean sauce over the whole length of the fish and place the shredded scallions on top. Serve garnished with cilantro leaves and lemon slices.

FISH STEAKS

If using fish steaks, rub them with the salt and sesame oil, but do not score with a knife. The fish may require less cooking, depending on the thickness of the steaks – test for doneness with a skewer after about 8 minutes.

STEP 1

STEP 2

STEP 3

STEP 4

CHICKEN FOO-YUNG

*Strictly speaking, a foo-yung dish (the name means white lotus petals)
should use egg whites only to create a very delicate texture. But most
people associate foo-yung with an omelet in Chinese restaurants.*

SERVES 4

6 oz chicken breast fillet, skinned
$\frac{1}{2}$ tsp salt
pepper
1 tsp rice wine or dry sherry
1 tbsp cornstarch
3 eggs, beaten
$\frac{1}{2}$ tsp finely chopped scallions
3 tbsp vegetable oil
1 cup green peas
1 tsp light soy sauce
salt
few drops of sesame oil

1 Cut the chicken across the grain
into very small, paper-thin slices,
using the cleaver. Place the slices in a
shallow dish, add the ½ teaspoon salt,
pepper, wine, and cornstarch and turn
in the mixture until they are well coated
and the mixture is smooth.

2 Beat the eggs in a small bowl with
a pinch of salt and the scallions.

3 Heat oil in a preheated wok, add
chicken slices and stir-fry for about
1 minute, making sure that the slices are
kept separated. Pour the beaten eggs
over the chicken, and lightly scramble

until set. Do not stir too vigorously, or
the mixture will break up in the oil. Stir
the oil from the bottom of the wok so that
the foo-yung rises to the surface.

4 Add the peas, salt and soy sauce
and blend well. Sprinkle with
sesame oil and serve.

VARIATION

If available, chicken *goujons* can be used
for this dish: these are small, delicate
strips of chicken which require no further
cutting and are very tender.

LEMON CHICKEN

Lemon sauce is a Cantonese specialty, easily available from Oriental stores, or you can make your own.

STEP 1

STEP 2

STEP 3

STEP 4

SERVES 4

12 oz chicken breast fillets, skinned
1 tbsp rice wine or dry sherry
salt and pepper
1 egg, beaten
4 tbsp all-purpose flour blended with 2 tbsp
   water
vegetable oil, for deep-frying
ready-made lemon sauce, or homemade sauce
   (see right)
slices of fresh lemon, to garnish

LEMON SAUCE:
1 tbsp vegetable oil
1 cup Chinese Stock (see page 76)
1 tbsp superfine sugar
1 tbsp lemon juice
1 tbsp cornstarch
1 tsp salt
1 tsp lemon rind

Heat the oil in a wok until hot, reduce the heat and add all the other ingredients. Blend well, then bring to the boil and stir until smooth.

1 Cut the chicken into thin slices and place in a shallow dish with wine, salt and pepper. Leave to marinate for 25-30 minutes.

2 Make a batter with the egg and flour paste. Place the chicken slices in the batter and turn to coat well.

3 Heat the oil in a wok or deep-fryer. Deep-fry the chicken slices until golden brown, remove with a slotted spoon and drain on paper towels. Cut the chicken slices into bite-sized pieces.

4 Heat about 1 tablespoon of oil in a wok or pan. Stir in the lemon sauce until well blended and pour evenly over the chicken. Garnish with lemon slices.

READY-MADE SAUCES

Many ready-made sauces are now available, and they are very useful if you are short of time. However, try to find time to make this homemade lemon sauce, which has a delicious fresh taste.

STEP 1

STEP 2

STEP 3

STEP 4

CHICKEN WITH BEAN SPROUTS

This is the basic Chicken Chop Suey to be found in almost every Chinese restaurant and takeout all over the world.

SERVES 4

4 oz chicken breast fillet, skinned
1 tsp salt
¼ egg white, lightly beaten
2 tsp cornstarch paste (see page 77)
about 1 ¼ cups vegetable oil
1 small onion, thinly shredded
1 small green bell pepper, cored, seeded and
   thinly shredded
1 small carrot, thinly shredded
1⅓ cups fresh bean sprouts
½ tsp sugar
1 tbsp light soy sauce
1 tsp rice wine or dry shrerry
2-3 tbsp Chinese Stock (see page 76)
a few drops of sesame oil
chili sauce, to serve

1 Thinly shred the chicken and mix with a pinch of the salt, the egg white and cornstarch paste.

2 Heat the oil in a preheated wok and stir-fry the chicken for about 1 minute, stirring to separate the shreds. Remove with a slotted spoon and drain on paper towels.

3 Pour off the oil, leaving about 2 tablespoons in the wok. Add all the vegetables except the bean sprouts and stir-fry for about 2 minutes, then add the bean sprouts and stir for a few seconds.

4 Add the chicken with the remaining salt, sugar, soy sauce and wine, blend well and add the stock or water. Sprinkle with the sesame oil and serve at once.

CHICKEN CHOP SUEY

Chop Suey actually originated in San Francisco at the turn of the century when Chinese immigrants were first settling there, and was first devised as a handy dish for using up leftovers.

STEP 1

STEP 2

STEP 3

STEP 4

CHICKEN WITH MUSHROOMS

Dried Chinese mushrooms should be used for this dish – otherwise use black rather than white fresh mushrooms.

SERVES 4

10-12 oz chicken, boned and skinned
½ tsp sugar
1 tbsp light soy sauce
1 tsp rice wine or dry sherry
2 tsp cornstarch
4-6 dried Chinese mushrooms, soaked in
*   warm water*
1 tbsp finely shredded ginger root
salt and pepper
a few drops of sesame oil
cilantro leaves, to garnish

1 Cut the chicken into small bite-sized pieces and place in a bowl. Add the sugar, soy sauce, wine, and cornstarch and leave to marinate for 25-30 minutes.

2 Drain the mushrooms and dry on paper towels. Slice the mushrooms into thin shreds, discarding any hard pieces of stem.

3 Place the chicken pieces on a heat-proof dish that will fit inside a bamboo steamer. Arrange the mushroom and ginger shreds on top of the chicken and sprinkle with salt, pepper, and sesame oil.

4 Place the dish on the rack inside a hot steamer or on a rack in a wok filled with hot water and steam over high heat for 20 minutes. Serve hot, garnished with cilantro leaves.

CHINESE MUSHROOMS

Chinese mushrooms come in many varieties: Shiitake are the best, and the two terms are often used synonymously. These fragrant mushrooms are most readily available at Oriental food stores and supermarkets but are also seasonally available.
Do not throw away the soaking water from the dried Chinese mushrooms. It is very useful, as it can be added to soups and stocks to give extra flavor.

STEP 1

STEP 2

STEP 3

STEP 4

DUCK WITH PINEAPPLE

For best results, use ready-cooked duck meat, widely available from Chinese restaurants and takeouts.

SERVES 4

about 1 cup cooked duck meat
3 tbsp vegetable oil
1 small onion, thinly shredded
2-3 slices ginger root, thinly shredded
1 scallion, thinly shredded
1 small carrot, thinly shredded
2/3 cup canned pineapple chunks
1/2 tsp salt
1 tbsp red rice vinegar
2 tbsp syrup from the pineapple
1 tbsp cornstarch paste (see page 77)
black bean sauce, to serve (optional)

1 Cut the cooked duck meat into thin strips.

2 Heat the oil in a preheated wok, add the shredded onion and stir-fry until the shreds are opaque. Add the ginger, scallion and carrot shreds. Stir-fry for about 1 minute.

3 Add the duck shreds and pineapple to the wok with the salt, rice vinegar, and the pineapple syrup. Stir until the mixture is blended well.

4 Add the cornstarch paste and stir for 1-2 minutes until the sauce has thickened. Serve hot.

CANNED PINEAPPLE

Fortunately, most canned fruit is now available preserved in juice rather than syrup. The sugared syrup once used exclusively for this purpose was cloyingly sweet. To prepare this dish, be sure to choose pineapple in juice rather than syrup, so that the sauce is pleasantly tangy rather than overwhelmingly sugary.

RED RICE VINEGAR

Red rice vinegar is made from fermented rice. It has a distinctive dark color and depth of flavor. If unavailable, use red wine vinegar, which is similar in flavor.

STEP 1

STEP 2

STEP 3

STEP 4

STIR-FRIED PORK WITH VEGETABLES

This is a basic "meat and vegetables" recipe – the meat can be pork, chicken, beef or lamb, and the vegetables can be varied according to taste or availability.

SERVES 4

8 oz boneless pork, sliced
1 tsp sugar
1 tbsp light soy sauce
1 tsp rice wine or dry sherry
1 tsp cornstarch paste (see
    page 77)
1 small carrot
1 small green bell pepper, cored and seeded
about 1½ - 2 cups Chinese cabbage
4 tbsp vegetable oil
1 scallion, cut into short sections
a few small slices of peeled ginger root
1 tsp salt
2-3 tbsp Chinese Stock (see page 77) or
    water
a few drops of sesame oil

1 Thinly slice the pork into small pieces and place in a shallow dish. Add half the sugar and the soy sauce, the wine, and cornstarch paste, and leave in the refrigerator to marinate for 10-15 minutes.

2 Cut the carrot, green bell pepper and Chinese cabbage into thin slices roughly the same length and width as the pork pieces.

3 Heat the oil in a preheated wok and stir-fry the pork for about 1 minute to seal in the flavor. Remove with a slotted spoon and keep warm.

4 Add the carrot, bell pepper, Chinese cabbage, scallion and ginger and stir-fry for about 2 minutes.

5 Add the salt and remaining sugar, followed by the pork and remaining soy sauce, and the stock or water. Blend well and stir for another 1-2 minutes until hot. Sprinkle with the sesame oil and serve.

ALTERNATIVES

This dish can be made with other meats, as mentioned in the introduction. If using chicken strips, reduce the initial cooking time in the wok.

STEP 1

STEP 2

STEP 3

STEP 4

SWEET-&-SOUR PORK

This has to be the most popular Chinese dish all over the world.
The pork can be replaced with almost any other ingredient:
fish, shrimp, chicken, or even vegetables.

SERVES 4

8-10 oz lean pork
2 tsp brandy or whisky
vegetable oil, for deep-frying
1 egg, beaten
2 tbsp all-purpose flour
salt and pepper

SAUCE:
1 tbsp vegetable oil
1 small onion, diced
1 small carrot, diced
½ small green bell pepper, cored, seeded and
  diced
1 tbsp light soy sauce
3 tbsp sugar
3 tbsp wine vinegar
1 tbsp tomato paste
about 3-4 tbsp Chinese Stock (see page 76)
  or water
1 tbsp cornstarch paste (see page 77)

1 Cut the pork into small bite-sized cubes. Place in a dish with the salt, pepper and brandy and leave to marinate for 15-20 minutes.

2 Heat the oil in a wok or deep-fryer. Place the pork cubes in a bowl with the beaten egg and turn to coat. Sprinkle on the flour and turn the pork cubes until they are well coated.

3 Deep-fry the pork cubes in batches for about 3-4 minutes, stirring gently to separate the pieces. Remove with a slotted spoon or strainer and drain on paper towels. Reheat the oil until hot, and return the meat to the wok for another minute or so or until golden brown. Remove with a slotted spoon and drain on paper towels.

4 To make the sauce, heat the oil in a preheated wok or pan, add the vegetables and stir-fry for about 1 minute. Add the seasonings and tomato paste with stock or water, bring to the boil and thicken with the cornstarch paste.

5 Add the pork and blend well so that each piece of meat is coated with the sauce. Serve hot.

SPARE RIBS WITH CHILI

For best results, chop the spare ribs into small bite-size pieces.

STEP 1

SERVES 4

500 g/ 1 lb pork spare ribs
1 tsp sugar
1 tbsp light soy sauce
1 tsp rice wine or dry sherry
1 tsp cornstarch
about 2 ½ cups vegetable oil
1 garlic clove, finely chopped
1 scallion, cut into short sections
1 small hot chili pepper (green or red),
   thinly sliced
2 tbsp black bean sauce
about ⅔ cup Chinese Stock (see page 76)
   or water
1 small onion, diced
1 medium green bell pepper, cored, seeded
   and diced

1 Trim excess fat from the ribs, and chop each one into 3-4 bite-sized pieces. Place the ribs in a shallow dish with the sugar, soy sauce, wine, and cornstarch and leave to marinate for 35-45 minutes.

2 Heat the oil in a preheated wok. Add the spare ribs and deep-fry for 2-3 minutes until light brown. Remove with a slotted spoon and drain on paper towels.

3 Pour off the oil, leaving about 1 tablespoon in the wok. Add the garlic, scallion, chili pepper, and black bean sauce and stir-fry for 30-40 seconds.

4 Add the spare ribs, blend well, then add the stock or water. Bring to the boil, then reduce the heat, cover and braise for 8-10 minutes, stirring once or twice.

5 Add the onion and green bell pepper, increase the heat to high, and stir uncovered for about 2 minutes to reduce the sauce a little. Serve hot.

STEP 2

STEP 3

HANDLING CHILIES

Be very careful when handling and cutting chili peppers, as they exude a juice which can cause irritation of the skin. Be sure to wash your hands after handling, and keep well away from face and eyes. It is the seeds of the chili that are the hottest part – remove seeds if you do not want a very hot dish.

STEP 5

STEP 1

STEP 2

STEP 3

STEP 4

OYSTER SAUCE BEEF

Like Stir-fried Pork with Vegetables (page 48), the vegetables used in this recipe can be varied as you wish.

SERVES 4

10 oz beef steak
1 tsp sugar
1 tbsp light soy sauce
1 tsp rice wine or dry sherry
1 tsp cornstarch paste (see
   page 77)
$^{1}/_{2}$ small carrot
$^{2}/_{3}$ cup snow peas
$^{1}/_{3}$ cup canned bamboo shoots
1 cup canned straw mushrooms
about 1$^{1}/_{4}$ cups vegetable oil
1 scallion, cut into short sections
2-3 small slices ginger root
$^{1}/_{2}$ tsp salt
2 tbsp oyster sauce
2-3 tbsp Chinese Stock (see page 76)
   or water

1 Cut the beef into small, thin slices. Place in a shallow dish with the sugar, soy sauce, wine, and cornstarch paste and leave to marinate for 25-30 minutes.

2 Slice the carrots, snow peas, bamboo shoots and straw mushrooms so that as far as possible the vegetable pieces are of uniform size and thickness.

3 Heat the oil in a preheated wok and add the beef slices. Stir-fry for about 1 minute, then remove with a slotted spoon and keep warm.

4 Pour off the oil, leaving about 1 tablespoon in the wok. Add the sliced vegetables with the scallion and ginger and stir-fry for about 2 minutes. Add the salt, beef, and the oyster sauce with stock or water. Blend well until heated through, and serve with a dip sauce, if liked.

VARIATIONS

You can use whatever vegetables are available for this dish, but it is important to get a good contrast of color – don't use all red or all green for example.

54

CHAPTER FOUR

Vegetables

Being basically an agricultural country, China has really perfected vegetable cooking into a fine art – almost all are cooked for a very short time, thus preserving their natural flavor and texture, as well as the vitamins and the brightness of their colors.

The Chinese eat far more vegetables than meat or poultry, and with a few exceptions, almost all meat and poultry dishes include some kind of vegetable as a supplementary ingredient – the idea being to give the dish a harmonious balance of color, aroma, flavor and texture.

When selecting vegetables for cooking, the Chinese attach great importance to the freshness of ingredients used. Always buy crisp, firm vegetables, and cook them as soon as possible. Another point to remember is to wash the vegetables just before cutting, in order to avoid losing vitamins in water, and to cook them as soon as they have been cut so that the vitamin content is not lost through evaporation.

Opposite: *A stallholder in Mongolia proudly displays his selection of fruit and vegetables. Chinese cooks attach great importance to freshness, and visit the market daily to buy fresh produce for the family meal.*

STEP 1

STEP 2

STEP 3

STEP 4

STIR-FRIED MIXED VEGETABLES

The Chinese never mix ingredients indiscriminately – they are carefully selected to achieve a harmonious balance of contrasting colors and textures.

SERVES 4

²/₃ oz snow peas
1 small carrot
1¹/₄ cups Chinese cabbage
1¹/₃ cups fresh bean sprouts
1 cup black or white mushrooms
¹/₃ cup canned bamboo shoots, rinsed
  and drained
3-4 tbsp vegetable oil
1 tsp salt
1 tsp sugar
1 tbsp oyster sauce or light soy sauce
a few drops of sesame oil (optional)
dip sauce, to serve (optional)

1 Prepare the vegetables: cut the ends off the snow peas and remove any strings. Cut the carrot, Chinese cabbage, mushrooms and bamboo shoots into roughly the same shape and size as the snow peas.

2 Heat the oil in a preheated wok, and add the carrot first. Stir-fry for a few seconds, then add the snow peas and Chinese cabbage and stir-fry for about 1 minute.

3 Add the bean sprouts, mushrooms, and bamboo shoots and stir-fry for another minute.

4 Add the salt and sugar, continue stirring for another minute, then add the oyster sauce or soy sauce, blend well, and sprinkle with sesame oil (if using). Serve hot or cold, with a dip sauce, if liked.

OYSTER SAUCE

This sauce, made from oysters cooked together with salt and spices, is used in many Cantonese dishes. It is worth spending a little more on a good bottle of oyster sauce, as the more expensive brands are noticeably better. Good oyster sauce has a rich, almost beefy flavor. Once opened, a bottle of oyster sauce can be kept for months in the refrigerator and used to flavor a range of Oriental dishes.

BEAN SPROUTS

It is important to use fresh bean sprouts for this dish – the canned ones don't have the crunchy texture that is vital. If fresh ones are unavailable, select another vegetable, remembering to keep a color contrast.

STEP 1

STEP 2

STEP 3

STEP 4

BROCCOLI IN OYSTER SAUCE

Some Cantonese restaurants use only the stalks of the broccoli for this dish, for the crunchy texture.

SERVES 4

8-10 oz broccoli
3 tbsp vegetable oil
3-4 small slices ginger root
$^1\!/_2$ tsp salt
$^1\!/_2$ tsp sugar
3-4 tbsp Chinese Stock (see page 76) or
    water
1 tbsp oyster sauce

1 Cut the broccoli into small spears. Trim the stalks, peel off the rough skin, and cut the stalks diagonally into diamond-shaped chunks.

2 Heat the oil in a preheated wok and add the pieces of stalk and the ginger. Stir-fry for half a minute, then add the florets and continue to stir-fry for another 2 minutes.

3 Add the salt, sugar, and stock or water, and continue stirring for another minute or so.

4 Blend in the oyster sauce. Serve hot or cold.

BROCCOLI STALKS

The broccoli stalks have to be peeled and cut diagonally to ensure that they will cook evenly. If they are thin stalks, the pieces can be added to the wok at the same time as the buds, but otherwise add the stalks first, to ensure that they will be tender.

VARIATION

Any crunchy-textured vegetable can be used in this recipe. If preferred, you could use cauliflower, celery, zucchini, French beans, etc., making sure that they are cut into even-sized pieces.

BRAISED CHINESE VEGETABLES

This dish is also known as Lo Han Zhai or Buddha's Delight. The original recipe calls for no less than 18 different vegetables to represent the 18 Buddhas (Lo Han) – but 6-8 are usually quite acceptable.

STEP 1

STEP 2

Serves 4

¼ cup dried wood ears
1 cake tofu (bean curd), about 3 in square
⅔ cup snow peas
1¼ cups Chinese cabbage
1 small carrot
about 12 canned baby sweetcorn, drained
1½ cups canned straw mushrooms, drained
⅓ cup canned water chestnuts, drained
1¼ cups vegetable oil
1 tsp salt
½ tsp sugar
1 tbsp light soy sauce or oyster sauce
2-3 tbsp Chinese Stock (see page 76) or water
a few drops of sesame oil

1 Soak the wood ears in warm water for 15-20 minutes, then rinse and drain, discarding any hard bits, and dry on paper towels.

2 Cut the cake of tofu into about 18 small pieces. Cut the ends off the snow peas and remove any strings. Cut the Chinese cabbage and the carrot into slices roughly the same size and shape as the snow peas. Cut the baby sweetcorn, the straw mushrooms, and the water chestnuts in half.

3 Heat the oil in a preheated wok. Add the tofu and deep-fry for about 2 minutes until it turns slightly golden. Remove with a slotted spoon and drain on paper towels.

4 Pour off the oil, leaving about 2 tablespoons in the wok. Add the carrot, Chinese cabbage, and snow peas and stir-fry for about 1 minute.

5 Now add the sweetcorn, mushrooms and water chestnuts. Stir gently for 2 more minutes, then add the salt, sugar, soy sauce, and stock or water. Bring to the boil and stir-fry for 1 more minute.

6 Sprinkle with sesame oil and serve hot or cold.

STEP 3

WOOD EARS

Wood ears (a kind of fungus) can usually be obtained in Chinese supermarkets. If unavailable, use another variety of Chinese mushrooms.

STEP 5

STEP 1

STEP 2

STEP 3

STEP 4

STIR-FRIED BEAN SPROUTS

Be sure to use fresh bean sprouts, rather than the canned variety, for this crunchy-textured dish.

SERVES 4

$2^2/_3$ cups fresh bean sprouts
2-3 scallions
1 medium red chili pepper (optional)
3 tbsp vegetable oil
$^1/_2$ tsp salt
$^1/_2$ tsp sugar
1 tbsp light soy sauce
a few drops of sesame oil (optional)

1 Rinse the bean sprouts in cold water, discarding any husks or small pieces that float to the top. Drain well on paper towels.

2 Cut the scallions into short sections. Thinly shred the red chili pepper, if using, discarding the seeds.

3 Heat the oil in a preheated wok. Add the bean sprouts, scallions and chili pepper, if using, and stir-fry for about 2 minutes.

4 Add the salt, sugar, soy sauce, and sesame oil, if using, to the mixture in the wok. Stir well to blend. Serve hot or cold.

TO GROW BEAN SPROUTS

It is very easy to grow bean sprouts. If you find it difficult to buy fresh ones, this could be the answer. Use dried mung beans, obtainable from supermarkets and health-food shops. Wash the beans thoroughly in several changes of water. Place in a lidded jar, or a seed sprouter if you have one, and place in a warm, dark place. Check daily and rinse with a little water to keep them moist. You should have sprouts ready to use in 3-4 days.

VARIATION

The red chili pepper gives a bite to this dish – leave the seeds in for an even hotter taste. If you prefer a milder, sweeter flavor use red bell pepper instead of the chili pepper. Core, seed and cut into strips in the same way.

CHAPTER FIVE

Rice and Noodles

Rice and noodles provide bulk in the Chinese diet, but the recipes given here are meant to be served on their own, as a light meal or a snack. For an everyday meal, plain rice is served with two or three other dishes – usually meat and vegetables together with a soup. Fried rice and chow mein are served only at formal occasions, or as a snack between main meals.

In China noodles are always served at birthday celebrations, as the Chinese consider that the length of noodles symbolizes long life.

The Chinese do not normally conclude an everyday meal with a dessert, but fresh fruit can always be served for those who are used to ending a meal with something sweet.

Opposite: A woman tends the irrigation system in rice paddy fields near Guilin. Rice is the most important staple in the Chinese diet and vast tracts of fertile land are given over to its cultivation.

STEP 1

STEP 3a

STEP 3b

STEP 5

SEAFOOD CHOW MEIN

*Use whatever seafood is available for this delicious noodle dish –
mussels or crab would also be suitable. Simply add to the
wok with the other seafood in step 6.*

SERVES 4

3 oz squid, cleaned
3-4 fresh scallops
$\frac{1}{2}$ cup raw shrimp, shelled
$\frac{1}{2}$ egg white, lightly beaten
1 tbsp cornstarch paste (see page 77)
$\frac{1}{2}$ lb egg noodles
5-6 tbsp vegetable oil
2 tbsp light soy sauce
$\frac{2}{3}$ cup snow peas
$\frac{1}{2}$ tsp salt
$\frac{1}{2}$ tsp sugar
1 tsp Chinese rice wine or dry sherry
2 scallions, finely shredded
a few drops of sesame oil

1 Open up the squid and score the inside in a criss-cross pattern, then cut into pieces about the size of a postage stamp.

2 Soak the squid in a bowl of boiling water until all the pieces curl up. Rinse in cold water and drain.

3 Cut each scallop into 3-4 slices. Cut the shrimp in half lengthwise if large. Mix the scallops and shrimp with the egg white and cornstarch paste.

4 Cook the noodles in boiling water according to the instructions on the package, then drain and rinse under cold water. Drain well, then toss with about 1 tablespoon of oil.

5 Heat 3 tablespoons of oil in a preheated wok. Add the noodles and 1 tablespoon of the soy sauce and stir-fry for 2-3 minutes. Remove to a large serving dish.

6 Heat the remaining oil in the wok and add the snow peas and seafood. Stir-fry for about 2 minutes, then add the salt, sugar, wine, remaining soy sauce, and about half the scallions. Blend well and add a little stock or water if necessary.

7 Pour the seafood mixture on top of the noodles and sprinkle with sesame oil. Garnish with the remaining scallions and serve hot or cold.

FRIED NOODLES (CHOW MEIN)

*This is a basic recipe for Chow Mein. Other ingredients, such as
chicken or pork can be added if liked.*

STEP 1

SERVES 4

¹/₂ lb egg noodles
3-4 tbsp vegetable oil
1 small onion, finely shredded
1 ¹/₃ cups fresh bean sprouts
1 scallion, finely shredded
2 tbsp light soy sauce
a few drops of sesame oil

1 Cook the noodles in salted boiling
water according to the instructions
on the package (usually no more than
4-5 minutes).

2 Drain and rinse the noodles in cold
water; drain well, then toss with a
little vegetable oil.

3 Heat the remaining oil in a
preheated wok. Stir-fry the onion
for about 30-40 seconds, then add the
bean sprouts and noodles, stir and toss
for 1 more minute.

4 Add the scallion and soy sauce, and
blend well. Sprinkle with the
sesame oil and serve.

FRESH NOODLES

Noodles are made from wheat or rice
flour, water and egg. Handmade noodles
are made by an elaborate process of
kneading, pulling and twisting the dough,
and it takes years to learn the art. Noodles
are a symbol of longevity, and so are
always served at birthday celebrations – it
is regarded as bad luck to cut them.

If fresh egg noodles are available, they
require very little cooking: simply place in
boiling water for about 3 minutes, then
drain and toss in oil. Noodles can be
boiled and eaten plain, or stir-fried with
meat and vegetables for a light meal
or snack.

STEP 2

STEP 3

STEP 4

STEP 1

STEP 2

STEP 3

STEP 4

SINGAPORE-STYLE RICE NOODLES

Rice noodles or vermicelli are also known as rice sticks. Egg noodles can be used for this dish, but it will not taste the same. The ideal meat to use is Barbecue Pork (see page 16).

SERVES 4

½ lb rice vermicelli
1 cup cooked chicken or pork
½ cup peeled shrimp, defrosted if frozen
4 tbsp vegetable oil
1 medium onion, thinly shredded
1⅓ cups fresh bean sprouts
1 tsp salt
1 tbsp mild curry powder
2 tbsp light soy sauce
2 scallions, thinly shredded
1-2 small fresh green or red chili peppers,
    seeded and thinly shredded

1 Soak the rice vermicelli in boiling water for 8-10 minutes, then rinse in cold water and drain well.

2 Thinly slice the cooked meat. Dry the shrimp on paper towels.

3 Heat the oil in a preheated wok. Add the onion and stir-fry until opaque. Add the bean sprouts and stir-fry for 1 minute.

4 Add the noodles with the meat and shrimp, and continue stirring for another minute.

5 Blend in the salt, curry powder and soy sauce, followed by the scallions and chili peppers. Stir-fry for one more minute, then serve immediately.

RICE NOODLES

Rice noodles are very delicate noodles made from rice flour. They become soft and pliable after being soaked for about 15 minutes. If you wish to store them after they have been soaked, toss them in a few drops of sesame oil then place them in a sealed container in the refrigerator.

VARIATION

For a really authentic flavor include 1 tablespoon dried shrimps, which have a strong, pungent taste. Soak in warm water for 30 minutes, drain and add to the noodles at step 4.

SPECIAL FRIED RICE

Special Fried Rice, sometimes called Yangchow Fried Rice, is almost a meal in itself. Make sure the cooked rice is completely dry and cold before adding it to the wok, otherwise it might stick and become lumpy.

STEP 1

SERVES 4

¹/₂ cup peeled shrimp
¹/₂ cup cooked meat (chicken, pork or ham)
1 cup green peas
3 eggs
1 tsp salt
2 scallions, finely chopped
4 tbsp vegetable oil
1 tbsp light soy sauce
1 tsp Chinese rice wine or dry sherry
    (optional)
4 cups cooked rice

scramble. Add the rice and stir to make sure each grain of rice is separated, then add the remaining salt and scallions, and the shrimp, meat, and peas. Blend well and serve hot or cold.

STEP 2

1 Dry the shrimp on paper towels. Cut the meat into small dice about the same size as the peas.

2 In a bowl, lightly beat the eggs with a pinch of salt and a few pieces of the scallions.

3 Heat 2 tablespoons of the oil in a preheated wok. Add the peas, shrimp, and meat, and stir-fry for about 1 minute. Stir in the soy sauce and wine, then remove and keep warm.

4 Heat the remaining oil in the wok and add the eggs. Stir to lightly

FRESH PEAS

Fresh peas straight from the shell really do make a difference to this dish. Their vivid, emerald color and just-off-the-vine flavor make it worth the (relatively small) amount of effort. Shell and lightly blanch the peas before stir-frying them.

PERFECT RICE

Cook the rice by the absorbtion method as described on page 78. Leave to stand, covered, until the rice has absorbed all the water, then turn out on to a large flat plate or baking sheet. Spread the rice out and leave until completely cold and dry.

STEP 3

STEP 4

CHINESE COOKING

CHINESE STOCK

This basic stock is used in
Chinese cooking not only as
the basis for soup-making, but
also whenever liquid is
required instead of plain water.

MAKES 10 CUPS

1½ lb chicken pieces
1½ lb pork spare ribs
15 cups cold water
3-4 pieces ginger root, crushed
3-4 scallions, each tied into a
*   knot*
3-4 tbsp Chinese rice wine or dry
*   sherry*

1. Trim off excess fat from the
chicken and spare ribs; chop
them into large pieces.

2. Place the chicken and pork
in a large pot with water; add
the ginger and scallion knots.

3. Bring to the boil, and skim
off the scum. Reduce heat and
simmer uncovered for at least
2-3 hours.

4. Strain the stock, discarding
the chicken, pork, ginger and
scallions; add the wine and
return to the boil, simmer for
2-3 minutes.

Refrigerate the stock when
cool; it will keep up to 4-5 days.
Alternatively, it can be frozen
in small containers and be
defrosted as required.

China is a vast country – about the same
size as the United States – and its climate
and food products are similarly varied.
Consequently, each region has a
distinctive style of cooking: no wonder
China can claim to have the world's most
diverse cuisine. Yet the fundamental
character of Chinese cooking remains the
same throughout the land: from Peking
in the north to Canton in the south, and
Shanghai in the east to Szechuan in the
west, different ingredients are prepared,
cooked and served in accordance with the
same centuries-old principles. Some of the
cooking methods may vary a little from
one region to another, and the emphasis
on seasonings may differ, but basically
dishes from different regions are all
unmistakably "Chinese".

The principles of Chinese cooking

What distinguishes Chinese cooking from
all other food cultures is the emphasis on
the harmonious blending of color, aroma,
flavor, and texture both in a single dish
and in a course of dishes for a meal.
Balance and contrast are the key words,
based on the ancient Taoist philosophy of
yin and yang. Consciously or
unconsciously, Chinese cooks from the
housewife to the professional chef all
work to this yin-yang principle:
harmonious balance and contrast in
conspicuous juxtaposition of different
colors, aromas, flavors and textures by
varying the ingredients, cutting shapes,
seasonings and cooking methods.

In order to achieve this, two most
important factors should be observed:
heat and timing – the degree of heat and
duration of cooking, which means the
right cooking method for the right food.
This is why the size and shape of the cut
ingredient must, first of all, be suitable
for a particular method of cooking. For
instance, ingredients for quick stir-
frying should be cut into small, thin
slices or shreds of uniform size, never
large, thick chunks. This is not just for
the sake of appearance, but also because
ingredients of the same size and shape
require about the same amount of time
in cooking.

EQUIPMENT AND UTENSILS

There are only a few basic implements
in the Chinese *batterie de cuisine* that are
considered essential in order to achieve
the best results. Equivalent equipment is
always available in a Western kitchen,
but Chinese cooking utensils are of an
ancient design, usually made of
inexpensive materials; they have been in
continuous use for several thousand of
years and do serve a special function.
Their more sophisticated and much
more expensive Western counterparts
prove rather inadequate in contrast.

Chinese cleaver An all-purpose cook's
knife that is used for slicing, shredding,
peeling, crushing and chopping.
Different sizes and weights are available.

Wok The round-bottomed iron wok

conducts and retains heat evenly, and because of its shape, the ingredients always return to the center, where the heat is most intense, however vigorously you stir. The wok is also ideal for deep-frying – its conical shape requires far less oil than the flat-bottomed deep-fryer, and has more depth (which means more heat) and more cooking surface (which means more food can be cooked at one time). A wok is also used for braising, steaming, boiling and poaching, etc. – in other words, the whole spectrum of Chinese cooking methods can be executed in a single utensil.

Ladle and spatula Some wok sets come with a pair of stirrers in the form of a ladle and spatula. Of the two, the flat ladle or scooper (as it is sometimes called) is more versatile. It is used by the Chinese cook for adding ingredients and seasonings to the wok as well as for stirring.

Strainers There are two basic types of strainers – one is made of copper or steel wire with long bamboo handles, the other of perforated iron or stainless steel. Several different sizes are available.

Steamers The traditional Chinese steamer is made of bamboo, and the modern version is made of aluminum. Of course, the wok can be used as a steamer with a rack or trivet and the dome-shaped wok lid.

Chopsticks Does Chinese food taste any better when eaten with chopsticks? This is not merely an aesthetic question, but also a practical point, partly because all Chinese food is prepared in such a way that it is easily picked up by chopsticks.

Learning to use chopsticks is quite simple and easy – place one chopstick in the hollow between thumb and index finger and rest its lower end below the first joint of the third finger. This chopstick remains stationary. Hold the other chopstick between the tips of the index and middle finger, steady its upper half against the base of the index finger, and use the tip of the thumb to keep it in place. To pick up food, move the upper chopstick with index and middle fingers.

GLOSSARY OF INGREDIENTS USED IN CHINESE COOKING

Baby sweetcorn Baby corn cobs have a wonderfully sweet fragrance and flavor, and an irresistible texture. They are available both fresh and canned.

Bamboo shoots Available in cans only. Once opened, the contents may be kept in fresh water in a covered jar for up to a week in the refrigerator.

Bean sprouts Fresh bean sprouts, from mung or soya beans, are widely available from Oriental stores and supermarkets. They can be kept in the refrigerator for two to three days.

Black bean sauce Sold in jars or cans. Salted beans are crushed and mixed with flour and spices (such as ginger, garlic or chili) to make a thickish paste. Once opened, keep in the refrigerator.

CORNSTARCH PASTE

Cornstarch paste is made by mixing 1 part cornstarch with about 1½ parts of cold water. Stir until smooth. The paste is used to thicken sauces.

SHRIMP WITH DIP SAUCE

1²/₃ cups raw shrimp, defrosted if frozen
1 tsp salt
4 cups water
2 scallions, shredded
2-3 slices ginger root, shredded
2 green or red chilies, seeded and finely shredded
1 tbsp vegetable oil
2 tbsp light soy sauce
1 tbsp red rice vinegar
1 tsp sesame oil

1. Poach the shrimp in boiling, salted water for 1 minute, then turn off the heat. Leave to stand for 1 minute, then remove with a slotted spoon and drain on paper towels.

2. Place the scallions, ginger, and chilies in a small heatproof bowl. Heat the oil until hot and pour into the bowl. Add the soy sauce, vinegar and sesame oil and stir well.

3. Shell the shrimp, leaving the tails, and arrange on a serving dish. Serve with the dip sauce.

PLAIN RICE

Use long-grain or patna rice,
or, better still, try fragrant
Thai rice.

SERVES 4
1 heaped cup long-grain rice
about 1 cup cold water
pinch of salt
1/2 tsp oil (optional)

1. Wash and rinse the rice just
once. Place the rice in a
saucepan and add enough
water so that there is no more
than ⅜ in of water above the
surface of the rice.

2. Bring to the boil, add salt
and oil (if using), and stir to
prevent the rice sticking to the
bottom of the pot.

3. Reduce the heat to very,
very low, cover and cook for
15-20 minutes.

4. Remove from the heat and
let stand, covered, for 10
minutes or so. Fluff up the rice
with a fork or spoon before
serving.

Chili bean sauce Fermented bean paste
mixed with hot chili and other
seasonings. Sold in jars, some sauces
are quite mild, but others are very hot.
You will have to try out the various
brands to see which one is to your taste.

Chili sauce Very hot sauce made from
chilis, vinegar, sugar, and salt. Usually
sold in bottles and should be used
sparingly in cooking or as a dip.
Tabasco sauce can be a substitute.

Chinese cabbage Also known as
Chinese leaves, there are two widely
available varieties. The most commonly
seen one is a pale green color and has a
tightly wrapped, elongated head –
about two-thirds of the cabbage is stem,
which has a crunchy texture. The other
variety has a shorter, fatter head with
curlier, pale yellow or green leaves, also
with white stems.

Cilantro Fresh cilantro leaves, also
known as Chinese parsley or coriander,
are widely used in Chinese cooking as a
garnish.

Dried Chinese mushrooms Highly
fragrant dried mushrooms, which add a
special flavor to Chinese dishes. There
are many different varieties, but
Shiitake are the best. They are not
cheap, but a small amount will go a
long way, and they will keep
indefinitely in an airtight jar. Soak
them in warm water for 20-30 minutes
(or in cold water for several hours),
squeeze dry, and discard the hard stalks
before use.

Egg noodles There are many varieties of
noodles in China, ranging from flat,
broad ribbons to long narrow strands.
Both dried and fresh noodles are
available.

Five-spice powder A mixture of star
anise, fennel seeds, cloves, cinnamon
bark and Szechuan pepper. It is very
pungent, so should be used sparingly. It
will keep in an airtight container
indefinitely.

Ginger root Fresh ginger root should be
peeled then sliced, finely chopped or
shredded before use. It will keep for
weeks in a dry, cool place. Dried ginger
powder is no substitute.

Hoi-sin sauce Also known as barbecue
sauce, this is made from soy beans,
sugar, flour, vinegar, salt, garlic, chili
and sesame seed oil. Sold in cans or jars,
it will keep in the refrigerator for several
months.

Oyster sauce A thickish soy-based sauce
used as a flavoring in Cantonese cooking.
Sold in bottles, it will keep in the
refrigerator for months.

Plum sauce Plum sauce has a unique,
fruity flavor – a sweet-and-sour sauce
with a difference.

Rice vinegar There are two basic types of
rice vinegar. Red vinegar is made from
fermented rice and has a distinctive dark
color and depth of flavor. White vinegar
is stronger in flavor, as it is distilled from
rice wine.

Rice wine Chinese rice wine, made from glutinous rice, is also known as "Yellow wine" (*Huang jiu* or *chiew* in Chinese), because of its golden amber color. The best variety is called Shao Hsing or Shaoxing from south-east China. A good dry or medium sherry can be an acceptable substitute.

Sesame oil Aromatic oil sold in bottles and widely used as a finishing touch, added to dishes just before serving. The refined yellow sesame oil sold in Middle-Eastern stores is not so aromatic, has less flavor and therefore is not a very satisfactory substitute.

Soy sauce Sold in bottles or cans, this popular Chinese sauce is used both for cooking and at the table. Light soy sauce has more flavor than the sweeter dark soy sauce, which gives the food a rich, reddish color.

Straw mushrooms Grown on beds of rice straw, hence the name, straw mushrooms have a pleasant slippery texture, and a subtle taste. Canned straw mushrooms should be rinsed and drained after opening.

Szechuan peppercorns Also known as *farchiew*, these are wild reddish-brown peppercorns from Szechuan. More aromatic but less hot than either white or black peppercorns, they do give a quite unique flavor to the food.

Szechuan preserved vegetables The pickled mustard root is very hot and salty. Sold in cans. Once opened, it should be stored in a tightly sealed jar in the refrigerator. It will keep for many months.

Tofu (bean curd) This custard-like preparation of puréed and pressed soya beans is exceptionally high in protein. It is usually sold in cakes about 3 in square and 1 in thick in Oriental and health-food stores. Will keep for a few days if submerged in water in a container and placed in the refrigerator

Water chestnuts The roots of the plant *Heleocharis tuberosa*. Also known as horse's hooves in China on account of their appearance before the skin is peeled off. They are available fresh or in cans. Canned water chestnuts retain only part of the texture, and even less of the flavor, of fresh ones. Will keep for about a month in the refrigerator in a covered jar, if you change the water every two or three days.

Wood ears Also known as cloud ears, this is a dried black fungus. Sold in plastic bags in Oriental stores, it should be soaked in cold or warm water for 20 minutes, then rinsed in fresh water before use. It has a crunchy texture and a mild but subtle flavor.

Yellow bean sauce A thick paste made from salted, fermented yellow soya beans, crushed with flour and sugar. It is sold in cans or jars, and once the can is opened, the sauce should be transferred to a screw-top jar. It will then keep in the refrigerator for months.

CHINESE FRUIT SALAD

The Chinese do not usually have desserts to end a meal, except at banquets and special occasions. Sweet dishes are usually served in between main meals as snacks, but fruit is refreshing at the end of a big meal.

1 cup crystal sugar
2½ cups boiling water
1 large honeydew melon
4-5 different fruits, such as pineapple, grapes, banana, mango, lychees or kiwi fruit

1. Dissolve the sugar in the boiling water, then leave to cool.

2. Slice 1 in off the top of the melon and scoop out the flesh, discarding the seeds. Cut the flesh into small chunks. Prepare the other fruits and cut into small chunks.

3. Fill the melon shell with the fruits and the syrup. Cover with plastic wrap and chill for at least 2 hours. Serve on a bed of crushed ice.

INDEX